Sports Illustrated
TABLE TENNIS

14/12 Budget '76

Sports Illustrated
TABLE TENNIS

By DICK MILES

Photographs
by Michael Louridas

J. B. LIPPINCOTT COMPANY
Philadelphia and New York

796.34

5

U.S. Library of Congress Cataloging in Publication Data

Miles, Dick.
   Sports illustrated table tennis.

   (The Sports illustrated library)
   1. Table tennis.   I. Sports illustrated (Chicago)
   II. Title.
   GV1005.M52 1974   796.34′6   74–5313
   ISBN–0–397–01024–9
   ISBN–0–397–01036–2 (pbk.)

Cover photograph: Al Freni

Photographs on pages 31, 43, 51, 55, 59, 71, 75, 81 and 83: Malcolm Anderson.

Photograph on page 65: *Table Tennis Topics* magazine.

Photograph on page 79: Donald M. Gunn.

Contents

Sports Illustrated
TABLE TENNIS

Introduction

TABLE TENNIS is, for me, one of those world-blotting-out activities, the ultimate escape. When I'm playing, temporal problems vanish. Only the ball exists. Moreover, it's a sport that can be enjoyed at any level of skill, from after-dinner addict to champion. It will keep you in shape until you are ninety, but it will devour your time. Be prepared for that. With a table-tennis craving in your soul, days are shorter—radically so.

Before we get down to a detailed analysis of championship stroking techniques, it might be appropriate to estimate just how much this book will improve your game. Obviously, not everyone will reach the same level; there are too many variables—basic aptitude, time given to practice and so on. But almost everyone should improve enough to become a winner against average players or, more precisely, against casual opponents—the kind you meet in your neighbor's rec room or in the traditional shipboard tournament.

Table tennis is so widely played as a pastime, as a game

rather than a sport (the industry spews out more than 500,000 tables a year and more than 10,000,000 rackets), that almost anyone with some understanding of the techniques used by world-class players is likely to become neighborhood champ at the very least. On the other hand, at its highest levels—a world championship, say, in London or Tokyo or Peking, where 500 players from 60 countries might compete—table tennis becomes a sport of superfast action demanding from its champions the same qualities that any great sport demands: speed, power, coordination, reflexes, stamina and, of course, physical fitness. At certain moments it also takes steel nerves and courage, the courage to attack the ball with full power, blasting it across the net at 100 mph when the score's against you 20 to 21.

You don't have to be a champion to enjoy table tennis or, indeed, to get hooked on it. It's also fair to say that in no other sport does a wider gap separate the untutored player from the expert. With few good models to emulate at the local level, most table-tennis players immediately develop habits that violate the fundamental principles of the game. This book is intended to correct this situation. However, I also feel certain that even relatively sophisticated players, those who have already joined clubs and played in their first sanctioned tournaments, will profit from it, for what I am going to present here are the basics of world-class technique.

1
Spin

LET'S BEGIN with a bit of theory: specifically, spin and what it means in the game. Actually, without spin there wouldn't be any such sport as table tennis, for it is only through spin that it becomes a power game. The ball weighs about ⅒ ounce, so you can easily see that any spin applied to it will greatly affect its trajectory, its flight path. Just as a baseball pitcher uses spins to deliver curves, sinkers and sliders, a table-tennis champion, though he uses less of a variety, controls every shot with spin. He even uses spin when he smashes away the high setup. If I were asked to pick out the single most important aspect of the game, I'd say without hesitation it was control of spin.

Though spin is used on every shot, and though the fine player frequently varies the *amount* of spin he imparts to the ball, the types of spin he can use effectively are limited to two: (1) a direct overspin, which rotates the ball toward his opponent and (2) a direct underspin, which rotates the ball away from his opponent. The overspin is called

11

topspin; the underspin is called chop. These two spins account for the classification of table-tennis players according to their styles. There are attackers and defenders. The attackers must control their shots with topspin; the defenders must use chop.

Actually, in the evolution of the modern high-speed game, more and more emphasis is being put on topspin and attacking play than on defense. Today probably 95 percent of the players you see at a world championship are attackers. This is not to say that defenders don't win. Lin Hui-ching, former women's world champion of China, and Tadeo Takashima, men's singles champion of Japan, are both defensive players. Though in the modern game a great disparity exists between the number of attackers and defenders, there is no disparity between their relative chances of winning. However, it is probably much harder to play a defensive game at world-class levels at the present time. The reason for this is inextricably bound up with the flat-surfaced sponge racket that just about every serious player in the world—attacker or defender—now uses. (The sponge racket will be discussed in Chapter 2.)

Attacking shots are made by imparting topspin to the ball. The effect of the spin is to tug the ball downward, to make it sink as it crosses the net. Without topspin, a powerfully hit shot would send the ball zooming far beyond the end of the table, like a line drive. The ball must *dip* as it crosses the net.

Now consider the defensive player's job. If he is to have any chance of returning a drive that is hurtling toward him at 100 mph, he will have to anticipate that drive and position himself far enough behind his end of the table, 15 feet perhaps, so that the ball's reduced velocity will make it easier to handle. Not only must he neutralize the ball's speed by being in the right place at the right time; he also has to read the topspin and allow for it in his stroke. When he has done all this—instantaneously and instinc-

12

tively, of course—his best chance of returning the ball and staying in the rally is to chop the ball back.

Unlike topspin, which gives the ball a steep downward trajectory, chop tends to maintain the ball's loft and keep it traveling on a straight course. The ball carries. At best, a fine chop shot will skim just a few inches above the net and then, as its forward motion dissipates, will settle with a low bounce onto the table.

Topspin for the attack and chop for the defense are virtually the only spins used in table tennis. Sidespin, a spin that rotates the ball laterally, is almost never used in the basic strokes of world-class players. If it is used at all, it is reserved for certain serves only. Sidespins are antithcorctical: they diminish the margin of error for both attack and defense without a corresponding increase in effectiveness.

2
Choosing a Racket and Other Equipment

BEFORE THE WHOLESALE CHANGEOVER to sponge rackets that occurred in the mid-1950's, it was common for a star player, after winning an important match or tournament, to be surrounded in the locker room by a cluster of hopefuls. Typically, they would ask, "Can you show me how you use your wrist on your forehand drive?" or, "Show me how you follow through on your backhand chop." But nowadays the first thing a champion is asked is, "What kind of sponge are you using? How thick is it? How grippy? How fast?"

Today's serious table-tennis players have gone somewhat "sponge crazy." They attribute their wins to their skill, but they blame their losses on the type of sponge they used. A lot of racket and sponge changing goes on, most of which is an exercise in futility.

THE RACKET

If you have recently taken up the game, or plan to, make sure that you buy sponge rackets. You must be modern.

Almost every sporting-goods department now carries an assortment of these. They are also in the mail-order catalogs of the big chain stores. The layer of sponge is usually about 2 mm thick and its playing surface may be either (1) flat and grippy, in which case it is called inverted sponge, or (2) covered with rubber pips similar to the basement-style rackets. The latter type is called sandwich sponge.

Although the Chinese team of the early '60s—who, in my opinion, were probably the greatest players the sport has ever seen—used sandwich sponge, it is likely that inverted sponge will be the only type of racket in table tennis within a few years. Even now, about 95 percent of the world-class players use it, and the Chinese players themselves, the last advocates of sandwich sponge, are switching to it more and more.

In America sponge rackets retail from $3 to $32. Even though differences in quality may not be obvious to the starting player, they do exist. The main difference is the speed and grippiness of the sponge; the faster and grippier, the more expensive. The type of wood that the racket is made of is relatively unimportant; it's the sponge that counts. At present, Japan is almost the only country producing table-tennis sponge. Other countries manufacture rackets, but they must import the sponge from Japan.

For the average player, I recommend choosing a racket in the middle- to upper-price range, around $7 to $10. The very cheap sponge rackets have only a small percentage of natural rubber in them and will not give you much catapult action. Nor will they give you the feel of sponge table tennis. At the high-priced end, the rackets are too fast for all but experts to control.

You should try to learn to control the ball with your *strokes*, not just your racket. If you can learn to attack, defend and control spin with a medium-fast sponge racket, your game will be that much more potent when you switch to the fastest sponge.

Apart from choosing in the medium-price range, you needn't look for much else when purchasing a bat, but you must make sure it feels comfortable in your hand with the playing grip I shall describe. Stick to name brands of rackets.

BALLS

The best come from Germany, Japan, Korea and England —and, when available, from China. To test a ball, spin it on a table with the seam up. If it wobbles, it will not play well. If it passes the roundness test, squeeze it in the middle by placing your thumb on one side of the seam and your forefinger on the other. It should give evenly.

TABLES

I think American tables are the best in the world. Made almost invariably of pressed wood, they give a much more uniform bounce than plywood. Moreover, the rougher surface texture of pressed wood makes the top more sensitive to spin. However, when buying a table, you should make sure that the top is not less than ¾ inch in thickness. Thinner tables yield too low a bounce. Also, don't ever polish your table with wax. The spin will not take afterward. To clean the table, use a damp rag only. A new table will rub; that is, the ball will pick up paint for a time.

This will lessen as the table is used, but don't try to speed up the process by using soap or abrasives.

APPAREL

I strongly urge you—whether you are a beginning, intermediate or advanced player—to wear tennis shoes, tennis shirt and shorts every time you play, even if it is just a practice session. You will feel more athletic, and the effort you have invested in changing will stimulate you to try harder. Remember, table tennis is a sport, not a parlor game.

3
The Grip

A GOOD GRIP goes hand in hand with good strokes. Unfortunately, all too many players have been thwarted in the climb up the ranking ladder by a fundamentally incorrect grip. What happens is that a poor grip forces the player to compensate for it in his stroke. The poorer the grip, the greater the compensation; the greater the compensation, the poorer the stroke.

THE SHAKEHANDS GRIP

Although the present world champions of men's and women's singles are both Chinese penholder-grip players, as, traditionally, most Oriental players have been, there has been a marked move toward the conventional Western shakehands grip in both China and Japan. Now about 30 percent of their players use the shakehands grip, and this includes many of their greatest international stars. Other than Asians, there are almost no world-class players who use the penholder grip. ;

Unquestionably, the penholder grip is better for the game's most important shot, the forehand drive. Thus, the high-powered Asian game relies almost exclusively on the forehand attack. But the shakehands grip, if properly used, is almost as good for the forehand attack and is certainly better for all other shots.

Therefore, I recommend the shakehands grip. For one thing, it is easier to use than the penholder grip; for another, it is more adaptable to the all-around game, attack *combined* with defense, which I really believe is the best style.

To form the correct shakehands grip, insert the racket into the web between your thumb and forefinger (see Figure 1).

FINGER POSITION

It is particularly important that the bat go as far down into the hand as possible. Here the racket itself can be a factor. Rackets with a wide, sloping "throat" (where the handle joins the blade) are harder to grip in this way. They have a tendency to slip upward out of the hand when any pressure is applied in the grip. Rackets with a narrow, squarer throat are therefore preferable.

The handle of the bat should cross the palm diagonally and should rest on the heel of the palm (see *a* of Figure 2). Held in this way, the bat will lie almost at right angles to the forefinger (see *b* of Figure 2). The bat should not be clenched in the fist; it is the fingers that hold it in place. You should have a feeling of tension but not of strain.

For me, the greatest tension is in the last two fingers, as these actually lock the bat into place. The thumb and forefinger serve mainly as a brace to keep the bat from swerving in the web. One reason for keeping the tension

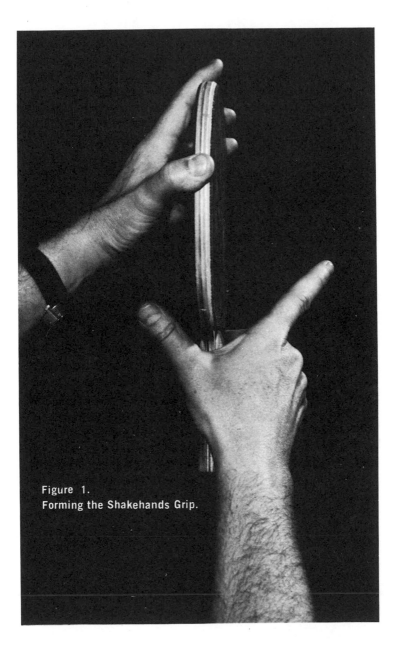

Figure 1.
Forming the Shakehands Grip.

Figure 2.
The Correct Shakehands Grip.

a Forehand Side.

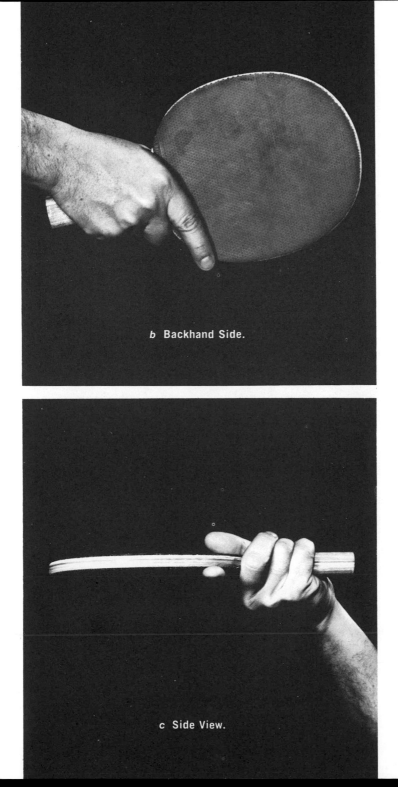

b Backhand Side.

c Side View.

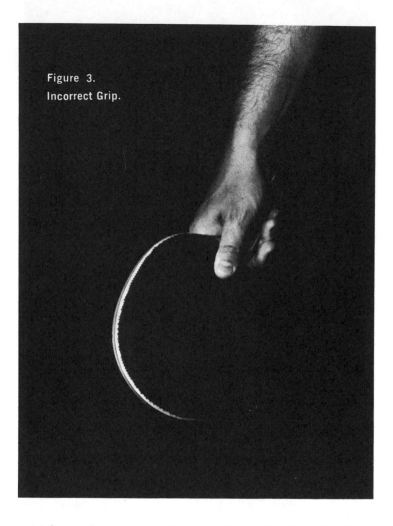

Figure 3.
Incorrect Grip.

mainly in the last two fingers is that this frees the head of the bat (the upper part) for rapid, whiplike motion. This implies wrist action in the strokes, which, indeed, there is. As you will see, the racket is never used as a mere extension of the arm. It's the head of the racket, activated by the flexible—but not slack—wrist (which is, in turn, integrated into the arm movement) that must do the work for you at the moment of impact when bat meets ball.

In *a* of Figure 2, you will see that my middle finger slightly overlaps the other two and that it is not completely resting on the handle. This overlapping is nothing more than an attempt to get the hand higher toward the blade. Try it. If it doesn't feel comfortable, there's nothing wrong with keeping the middle finger on the handle alongside the others.

One critical fine point in the grip, often overlooked even by experts, is this: when the grip has been made, none of the palp of the thumb should rest against the blade of the racket. In other words, don't leave your fingerprint on the rubber. (See Figure 3 for the *incorrect* thumb position.) Your thumb *must* lie so that your thumbnail is at right angles to the blade, as shown in *a* of Figure 2. Getting the flat of your thumb against the blade is dead wrong; that is a backhand grip. But since it is the forehand drive that is the big shot in table tennis, you should accommodate your grip to fit that shot. Moreover, you must maintain it, for exchanges are too fast to allow for grip switching during rallies.

4
The Push Strokes

THE STROKE MOST TAKEN FOR GRANTED in the champion's repertoire is the "push"—both backhand and forehand. Although the push is not a point-winning stroke, no one can play world-class table tennis without near perfection in his pushing game. In essence, the push is a waiting shot used merely to keep the ball in play. It is executed from a close-to-the-table position. The attacker uses it while jockeying into position to initiate his attack, whereas the defender uses it more passively.

Traditionally, the push was considered more important to the defender than to the attacker because it is really a miniature of the long-range chop, which is the backbone of defensive play. However, with the recent trend toward attacking as early in the point as possible, even on the service, it now looks as if a consistent pushing game is also vital to the attacker. Typically, when two attacks play (and bear in mind that 95 percent of the players are attackers), they will serve to each other by keeping the ball as close to the net as possible. If the serve is short enough, there is little chance for the receiver to attack it. And so the receiver, no matter how good his attack is, must temporize with a push return. He too tries to keep the ball close to the net lest his return offer the server an easy opportunity to attack. Even so, the server is usually able to initiate his attack on either the receiver's first or second return. Most Japanese players build their games around what they call the third-ball attack or the fifth-ball attack.

In any case, since no one can survive in table tennis without a competent push or, as it is sometimes called, a table game, the push should be the first stroke you learn. You will find your task much easier if you use the "buddy" system—that is, if you learn with a player of your own ability. In that way, you can practice the particular shot being developed; each of you in turn will feed balls to the right part of the table. After all, if you are trying to learn a forehand push step by step, with emphasis on finding the proper form, it makes no sense to practice the shot against some unrelenting competitor whose sole object is to win, perhaps even by keeping the ball away from your forehand.

Therefore, in the following directions, assume that the ball is coming toward you in a path that makes it possible for you to execute the shot without a great deal of footwork. (See page 40 for a discussion of footwork.)

THE READY POSITION

Assume that it is your opponent's serve. (Forget for the moment that in this case your opponent is your buddy.)

You must be prepared to receive any serve, and for that purpose there is a standard ready position in table tennis, just as there is in lawn tennis.

Position *a* of Figure 4 is the correct ready position for returning serves. As the term implies, you are ready to return serves made to either your backhand or your forehand. You should be standing about 2 feet behind your end of the table, with your feet about shoulder-width apart. Your weight is carried slightly forward, but it is evenly distributed over the flat surfaces of your feet. With your knees bent slightly forward, you have the feeling that you are sitting down a bit. You should be perfectly relaxed (but alert) and your arms should hang loosely from your shoulders, which should be slightly slouched and concave.

Extend the racket in front of you about 8 inches and hold it waist high. The faces of the racket blade are perpendicular; the handle of the racket is pointed slightly downward, which, in turn, points the head of the racket up a bit. This is an important checkpoint, for if your racket head is pointed upward, your wrist will be slightly cocked. And it *should* be. Also crucial is the position of your right forearm. (All instruction is geared to right-handed players; left-handers, of course, reverse.) It should be angled, from elbow to hand, toward your left, so that the racket is in the middle of your body with its top edges pointed directly at your opponent. This means that the wrist, as well as being cocked slightly upward, is also cocked back, so that there is a slight angle, a V, between the back of your racket hand and your forearm.

Your left hand is important in all your strokes, as it acts as the counterbalance that enables you to shift your weight smoothly, particularly for lateral movements. Right at the beginning you must learn to carry your left hand *high*. Always try to carry your wrist above your elbow. Among fine players, the wrist of the free hand seems to dangle independently.

THE BACKHAND PUSH

From this basic ready position, you should now be able comfortably to execute your first championship-looking table-tennis stroke. It will be the backhand push. (You know it's going to be the backhand because you've told your buddy to serve the ball to you, medium speed, directly down the center of the table.)

As the ball approaches, there is no transition to some special backhand push position; from the ready position you will move directly into the beginning of your backswing. And the backswing, in all table-tennis strokes, must be considered *part* of the stroke and be executed just as correctly as the part of the stroke that leads to impact.

Positions *b* and *c* in Figure 4 show the backswing for the backhand push leading out of the ready position for service return. You should have the feeling not so much of a swing but of a fluid, rhythmical drawing back of the racket. This drawing back is smooth and unhurried. Your racket, wrist and forearm should move back simultaneously. The motion is merely a swivel of the forearm in the elbow socket. You should draw your racket back on a constant horizontal plane until it almost touches your waist.

You will notice that between *a* and *c* the bat has been opened somewhat; that is, the angle of the blade has been tilted upward. With the bat at this angle, the ball will move slightly upward as it leaves the racket. It will also carry a bit of backspin.

From *d* the stroke moves into the forward swing. There is no pause between the limit of the backswing and the initiation of the forward swing. With the face of the blade still open, *push* the bat forward into the path of the oncoming ball. I stress push because at the moment of impact, position *e*, you must resist any urge to slap, tap or jerk your racket into the ball. The stroke is called a push, and you should make it that by trying to "hold" the ball on your racket as long as possible. In a sense, you should try to carry it over the net. Indeed, if you make the shot correctly, you will barely feel the impact. You are merely intercepting the ball midway between backswing and follow-through.

Position *h* is the full follow-through position. The follow-through must be a part of an uninterrupted stroke. Pay particular heed to your forearm, which should now be *fully* extended. Your racket head, still up, as it was throughout the stroke, should now point directly toward the net.

The backhand push may be one of the most important strokes in table tennis. Take time to learn it correctly. Don't compromise. You are not learning this shot just because you want to get the ball over the net; it is a miniature of what your backhand defense will be.

Apart from warning you against the temptation to tap or jerk the ball at impact, I also want to stress that the push is a passive shot. It is not supposed to be a point winner. The object is steadiness. Therefore, don't try to score points with the push by trying for more backspin than the natural open face of the racket gives you. The wrist action is only as much as is required to keep the stroke flowing smoothly.

30

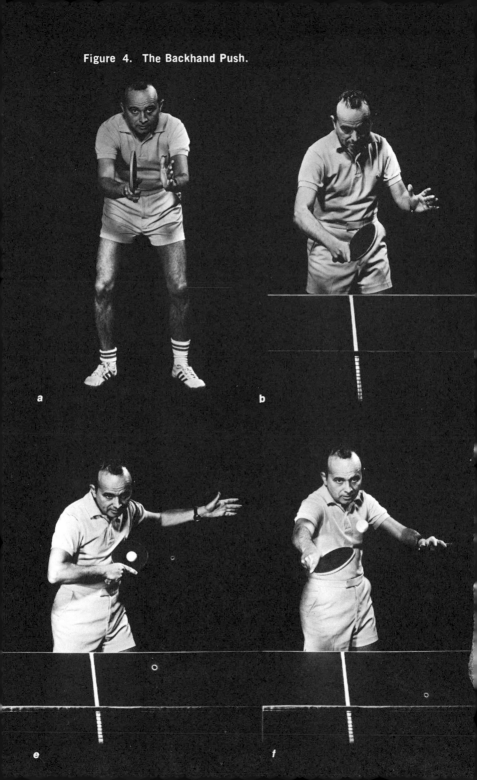

Figure 4. The Backhand Push.

a

b

e

f

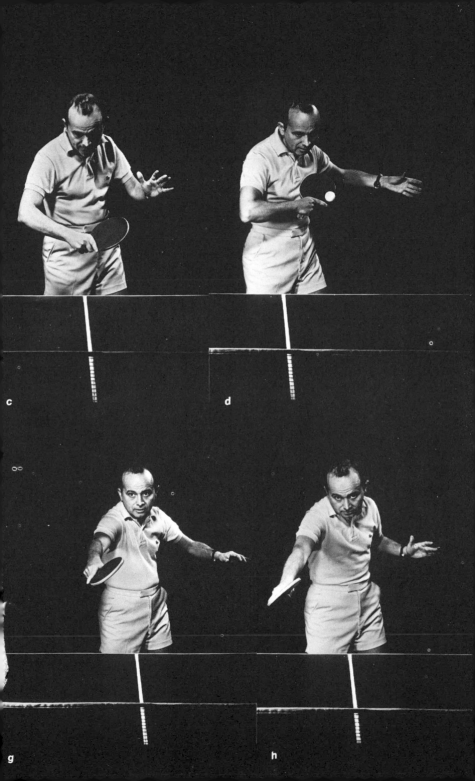

c   d

g   h

THE FOREHAND PUSH

After you have achieved some degree of proficiency in the backhand push—and let's say you and your buddy can keep the ball in play for something like 50 times across the net without missing—your next goal will be the forehand push. The forehand is somewhat more difficult than the backhand because it calls for some body pivot.

Here are the essentials of the stroke:

Once again it begins from the ready position; you should reach position *b* in Figure 5, which shows the initiation of the backswing, by a smooth body flow from the basic ready position, *a*.

In *b*, you see that as the racket has been taken back—and, again, it is drawn back, not swung back—there has been a simultaneous turning of the upper torso from left to right. This is the pivot, and it is very important because it allows you to transfer your weight smoothly throughout the swing. To understand the pivot, you should try to visualize the entire twisting action of hips and shoulders as revolving around your head; that is, while neck and head remain relatively in place, your hips and shoulders twist around that central axis. As this happens, some—*but not all*—of your weight transfers from your left side to your right. If all your weight transfers, the pivot will become a lunge and you will lose your balance.

Throughout the continuation of the backswing (*b* through *d*), you should be sure to keep your elbow well forward of your body. In a sense, your elbow doesn't move from where it was in the basic ready position. It is your right shoulder that, during the pivot, drags the forearm and elbow along with it as it moves to the right. Your left hand, remaining high, moves to the right and maintains approximately the same distance and relationship to your right hand that it had in the ready position.

Throughout the backswing, you should have the feeling that your *racket*, not your elbow, is being drawn back.

34

Figure 5. The Forehand Push.

a

b

e

f

c   d

0

g   h

Moreover, the head or top edge of the racket goes back first. It leads the way on the backswing, and it will retrace that same path on the forward swing.

The backswing illustrations also show that the angle of the bat has opened gradually. This is achieved by a slight cocking of the wrist—integrated, not independent, just as it was on the backhand push. ·

Once again you are going to strike the lower half of the ball, and the path of your swing will continue down through that lower half. The effect will be that the ball will carry backspin on it.

Positions *e* through *h* show the forward swing and follow-through. Notice in *g*, the position that was reached just after the contact point, that the wrist, from its slightly cocked position in the previous stages, has returned to a natural straight-line position relative to the forearm. Properly timed, this turning of the wrist insures that at impact the blade will be square to the point of aim. The wrist action is a controlled movement, not a snap.

The feeling you should have throughout the forward swing—and it is a controlled swing more on the order of a push or shove—is that your forearm is moving at one steady pace into the ball. Meanwhile, your wrist, which on the backswing had been slightly cocked, must now catch up with your forearm in order to be in line with it at the point of impact. Again, you should have absolutely no feeling of jerk or tap at impact.

Position *h* is the full follow-through position. It is crucial that you reach this position accurately because it demonstrates whether or not the entire path of your stroke was correct. When you have completed the follow-through, your upper arm, your forearm and your wrist should all be pointing in one continuous line. Your forearm has been extended, and if there is any bend at your elbow, it should be only very slight. To be certain that your wrist has moved during the shot, make sure that your thumb is also on a straight line with your arm. It should not be pointed to the right at the end of the follow-through.

Learning the push shots correctly will greatly increase your long-term chances of improvement to a high level, for all the essentials of the advanced strokes—timing, coordination and ball control—are factors in the push.

TIMING

There is no good way to teach timing. Some people have built-in timers, or "a sense of ball"; others will have to work hard at it. However, here are a few guidelines that may be helpful:

On every stroke, timing begins with the backswing. In essence, the backswing is a tracking device. As the ball approaches, you are, by means of the backswing, projecting the flight path it will take, judging its speed. (The faster the approach, the faster your backswing.) In other words, the backswing enables you to enter into the ball's rhythm. You must also anticipate the general direction of the ball —even before your opponent hits it. His body position should indicate the ball's flight path.

There is no general rule governing the speed of the backswing. Champions, even though their strokes are grooved from backswing to follow-through, can often hurry a backswing if necessary and still recover to make a fine shot. But a good guide for intermediate players is to make the tempo of the backswing coincide with the tempo of the approaching ball.

Another useful tip: Don't try to hit the ball on the top of the bounce. Actually, it is theoretically incorrect to do so. Better timing and control can be achieved if the ball is hit *just after* the top of the bounce. On the push shots, you should have the feeling that the ball is *falling*

39

onto your inward-moving racket. Try to visualize a small hoop, let's say the size of a saucer, lying in space horizontally about net high on your side of the table. You should hit the ball *just after* it drops through that hoop.

FOOTWORK

Good footwork is another natural gift that is almost impossible to teach in a book. Each player's footwork is unique and, without seeing the particular player in action, I cannot give any specific rules.

However, proper footwork is just as vital to good play as correct strokes and timing. If you reach the ball too late (or too early, as in most cases), you will have to readjust both timing and footwork to suit that particular shot. And while this recovery can often be made, it is not the best method. Ideally, your legs should move you into position with such precision that your stroke—which is grooved and flowing—brings the bat into contact with the ball at the precise moment on its trajectory that you visualized when the ball left your opponent's racket. Your stroke is a fixed piston, or lever. Your legs place you in the right spot at the right time. If that happens, your game will look, and indeed be, effortless.

TIPS

Two last tips concerning the push shots:

(1) Your backhand push should cover more court than your forehand push. Since it doesn't require a body pivot, it's an easier shot to make. Therefore, as well as using it for all shots that go to your left, use it for shots that go to your middle. You can even use it for shots that go a bit beyond your middle—almost as far as your right hip.

(2) Always hit the ball in the very center of the racket, the "sweet spot."

5

The Forehand Drive
and the
Backhand Attack

YOU HAVE NOW MASTERED two basic shots, and with these alone, presuming you take the time (20 to 30 hours of practice on each wing) to groove them into consistency, you should have no trouble in subduing neighborhood competition. But you won't really be playing the sport until you put power into your game. And that's done with the forehand drive, the big bomb of table tennis.

THE FOREHAND DRIVE

There is no limit to how hard a table-tennis ball can be hit and still go onto the table. A champion, when he goes for the "winner" during a rally, unleashes into the ball every bit of power he can muster. There is no holding back when he tries the forehand putaway.

The longer your backswing, the more power you can achieve on your stroke. It is easy to see that the forehand side allows more backswing room than the backhand side, so it is not surprising that even world-class players, with few exceptions, do not hit the ball nearly as hard on the backhand drive as they do on the forehand.

The forehand drive is really a combination of two movements: (1) a forward motion directly into the ball for power and (2) a simultaneous upward grazing motion over the top of the ball that applies the topspin necessary to force the ball downward as it crosses the net.

The forehand that I advocate, and the most orthodox one stylistically, is shown in all its phases in Figure 6.

The Ready Position

Position *a* is the ready position: in a sideways stance, the left hip is toward the net. In actual play, however, you would rarely see a player *assume* a ready-waiting position because the ball travels back and forth so quickly that one stroke must flow to the next without pause.

The Backswing

Position *b* shows the beginning of the backswing. It is initiated by a smooth, rhythmical pivot of the hips and shoulders from left to right. Nothing is abrupt. At the same time, the wrist begins to drop so that the head of the bat starts to point downward. When it reaches the full backswing position, it is pointed almost straight down. But it must begin its descent at the start of the backswing. Also, at this point the wrist is cocked back slightly.

Position *c* shows the backswing developing evenly. The wrist continues its descent and cocks a bit more. The elbow, still bent, is tucked in close to the right hip. The pivot continues to shift the weight toward the right side, thus freeing the left foot to adjust the stance, if necessary, as the ball approaches.

42

Figure 6. The Forehand Drive.

e

f

j

k

Position *d* shows the completion of the backswing. The arm is almost fully extended behind the player, but it is neither rigid nor slack. At this point the ball should be approaching its contact point; the player, pivoted to the right, has to draw a left-eyed bead on the ball over his left shoulder.

The Wrist Position

The wrist should be fully cocked now, so that the back of the hand and the backhand face of the racket form a V relative to the forearm.

The wrist must also be *down*. It is this downward position of the racket before it approaches the ball that determines how much topspin you will be able to put on the ball, because the wrist will move from a down to an up position as it grazes over the top of the ball.

The Hands

Note that the left hand has worked with the right. As the right hand extends backward, the left hand has stretched slightly forward; as the racket hand drops, the left hand lifts higher. The left hand is the counterbalance to the right.

The Contact Point

When you have reached this full backswing position, the ball should be approaching its contact point. Bear in mind, however, that your racket must be well below the intended contact point, as you will swing it upward toward that point, much like a bowling stroke. There should be no pause between the top of the backswing and the beginning of the forward swing; it all flows together.

The initiation of the forward swing is shown in *e*. An important point here is that though the racket is now moving forward, it is not the arm, forearm or wrist that is moving it.

Rather, it is the body, uncoiling from the pivot with a twisting of the hips and shoulders to the left, that is *dragging* the upper arm. And so, in *e*, the relative positions of racket, wrist and forearm are much the same as they were in *d*, the end of the backswing.

Position *f* shows the final phase before impact. For the purposes of instruction, imagine that at this point the ball is stationary. It is waiting, teed up, as it were, at its ideal contact point on its trajectory. This contact point will vary according to your opponent's returns. On underspin returns —the push shots, or chops—the best contact point for the drives is just *after* the ball has reached the top of its bounce. When attacking topspin shots, or when counterdriving a drive, for instance, the best contact point is at the top of the bounce. But in this case, let's assume your opponent is hitting a push return so that you will be hitting the ball on its descent. As your racket moves in and up toward the ball, you should have the sensation that the ball is *falling* onto your racket.

At this point in the swing, position *e*, the forearm should be accelerating, swiveling upward in the elbow socket. Simultaneously, the wrist is moving smartly forward, from its cocked position, into the ball; in effect, it is a hinge that moves in and up at the same time.

The entire timing of the swing has been geared so that the maximum power can be released on impact. And when I speak of power, I don't mean that every drive is hit as hard as possible. I mean that for the power expended, you should achieve the maximum speed of the ball. Economy is essential, because without it you cannot really control the power.

At impact, the topspin that is applied is almost a natural result of the grazing motion. To be sure, there is an advanced shot called a loop, in which the entire emphasis is on the topspin, but first you must learn to execute a consistent drive. On the drive you should never have the feeling of rubbing the ball at impact. Instead, you should graze

47

over it smoothly with your bat. The speed and thinness of the grazing action will determine the amount of spin you put on the ball.

Moreover, you must maintain a balance between spin and power. The more spin you try for, the slower your drive will travel; the more speed you try for, the less spin you can get. Actually, the inward–upward motion of the drive is a compromise. A stroke path that is horizontal will give you maximum speed; a vertical path will give you maximum spin. But neither by itself is effective.

The Follow-through Position

Positions g through k show the correct path of the follow-through, which is an essential part of the stroke. The racket finishes with its edge at the center of the forehead. The salute position, as it is called, is the typical follow-through position for the world's greatest attacking players.

Caution: Do not take the racket across your body. A particularly subtle point, often overlooked even by experts, is that though the racket moves from right to left on this shot, it does not actually cross the chest. That's because, with proper execution, the chest turns with the shot. If, however, the pivot is held back, if the chest does not turn, the right-to-left arm motion will finish across the body. Such a stroke can never be effective.

Don't flip the top edge of the racket over as you stroke into the ball. Once you decide (at the beginning of the forward swing) the path the racket will take, the angle of the racket stays the same. The top edge leads the way until it reaches the follow-through position. There is no "turning over." This can be seen in k, where there is still a backward curve in the wrist.

The follow-through must be firm. On the backswing the arm is relaxed, but during the forward swing the tension increases. At impact, particularly, you should feel that your hand and wrist are driving the bat firmly through the ball.

48

But you must not let up the tension after impact. You should have the feeling of snapping your racket into the follow-through position.

After the follow-through, be sure that you return your racket to a neutral position, similar to *a* of Figure 6, in anticipation of the next shot. Beginners often fall into the habit of becoming immobilized when they reach the follow-through position. In any case, the stroke is not completed until you have returned to the neutral position.

Tips

The forehand attack is not easy to perfect. You will need a lot of practice, but here are a few tips that may speed things up:

Your first step probably should be to groove the swing in the air—a kind of shadow-stroking process. The fight with the moving ball is so difficult (really a problem independent of the proper stroke) that there is no point in tackling two problems at once. Once the swing from start to finish is functioning smoothly, then dealing with a moving ball is less apt to alter the proper stroke path.

When, after some initial shadow-stroking, you begin to practice your attack with the ball, don't try for too much power. Consistency should be your first goal. Increase the power as you gain control of the ball. You should at least get to the point where you can consecutively topspin 15 or 20 balls without missing.

THE BACKHAND ATTACK

Good as your forehand may become, you're going to need a backhand attack to go with it. After all, if your backhand side develops into a completely passive defensive shot (the push), your opponent need only place the ball there and your forehand, bomb though it may be, will never explode.

The backhand attack illustrated in Figure 7 is the one used by most of today's champions. It is a shorter and quicker stroke than the forehand, and it is the stroke most often used against a topspin return—in other words, against an opponent who is fighting you for the attack by attacking to your weak backhand side.

The Ready Position

You should be close to the table, almost up against it, and shifted to your left. In other words, you allow yourself more court to cover with your forehand.

Position *a* is the ready position. The bat is perpendicular to the table, almost resting on it.

The Contact Point

As the ball approaches (carrying topspin), the player takes a very short backswing so that the racket almost touches his waist. Also, the face of the racket closes somewhat so that it is angled downward toward the net. Aimed this way, the ball would go into the net were it not for the fact that the opponent has hit it with topspin. The downward angle compensates for the topspin—but the angle itself must be adjusted on every shot according to the severity of the spin; the more spin, the steeper the downward angle.

In *b* the player is moving his racket back with the approaching ball. Note particularly that the elbow is well extended toward the net. On this shot, it remains in its original position; it is the hinge on which the forearm swings, and the forearm in turn is the hinge on which the wrist moves. The racket path of the forward swing is in, up and over the top surface of the ball. Unlike the forehand attack, the racket on the backhand changes angles during the swing, the top edge *turning over* the ball, smothering it to the extent required by the opponent's topspin.

50

Figure 7. The Backhand Attack.

a   b   c

d   e   f

Position *f* is the follow-through position. The stroke is short, and often it finishes abruptly with a little wrist snap that turns the racket head over the ball.

It is important on this shot to let the sponge do the work for you. Rather than feeling you are actually hitting the ball, you should feel that the ball is being catapulted off your racket. Also, the ball should be contacted *as it rises.* In a sense, it is trapped. Generally you make contact with the ball when it is lower than the net; therefore, it is difficult to get any real power explosion on the shot. But in the backhand attack, quickness of return is the goal. You don't want to give your opponent time to get his own forehand into use.

However, if your opponent gives you a weak or slow return, or if you have confidence that you can make the shot, what you should try to do is step back away from the table (as the ball approaches, of course, and not before your opponent has hit it) and give the ball a chance to rise to a higher point on its trajectory. In this case, since there is more clearance between the top of the net and your target, you can achieve more power via forearm and wrist snap. Or, better still, if you have the time, step around your backhand entirely—that is, move to your left—and slug your forehand.

The same backhand drive shown here can be made against returns carrying underspin. However, as experience will show you, the face of the racket will have to be opened (tilted up) as you bring it into the ball to compensate for the underspin. Remember, a ball approaching you with topspin will rise as it leaves your racket; an underspin ball will tend to head toward the net as it leaves your racket.

6

The Defense

THE DEFENSIVE STROKES are called chops because of the downward cleaving motion of the racket as it is swung in and down through the bottom surface of the ball. Choppers, players who are primarily defensive, are rare in world-class play these days—but not because the style is ineffective. On the contrary, whenever a good chopper appears, he or she turns in fine results. Germany's Eberhard Schöler, Japan's Tadeo Takashima and the Chinese women's world champions are all fine choppers. I myself chopped my way to third place in the world singles championship some years back, defeating along the way two members of the Chinese team and narrowly losing to another one in the semis, Jung Kuo-tuan, who went on to win it.

Why, despite these results, are there so few choppers at world championships? The answer is that defensive play is just too difficult for most players to master—not the defensive strokes themselves, but rather the mental discipline necessary to execute them under match conditions. For a chopper, the mental strain is enormous. The reason is that the grippy surface of the sponge bat gives the attacker—not necessarily a great attacker, just a good one—such a variation of spins, from superspin loop drives to ordinary topspin drives, often disguised, that the defensive player most often cannot really get into the game. Most of his effort is expended merely in reading the spin and readjusting his strokes with each chop he makes. If, by getting into a defensive groove during a match, he successfully begins to contain the attacker, he himself can begin to employ some of the tactics of defensive play: placement of the ball and, indeed, spin variations of his own. But most often the simple problem of reading the spin—which he must do with precision on every shot lest he miss outright or offer the attacker a complete setup—is the defender's undoing. After a while, the mental strain forces him into easy errors and he loses.

Thus, mental attitude is more important to the chopper than to the attacker. Forced back away from the table, sometimes as far as 15 to 18 feet, the chopper often feels at the complete mercy of the attacker. Only true grit overcomes this feeling.

Of course, every world-class player does, on occasion, chop. There are certain shots that can't be handled any other way. Thus, learning the defensive shots does not commit you to being a defensive player. Actually, they are musts in the repertoire of strokes.

As to which is basically the better style, attack or defense, my own opinion is that the ideal player of the future will be one who can attack and defend with equal skill. Such a player would have two ways of winning a match rather than one. He could actually change a losing game, an axiom that applies to table tennis just as it applies to any other sport.

Earlier I said that the push shots are really miniatures of the chopping stroke. Therefore, if you have achieved some mastery over the pushes previously illustrated, you should have little trouble acquiring control over the backhand and forehand chop. The main difference between the chops and the pushes is that in the chops you take a longer backswing and put more spin on the ball. Also, whereas the push is used against slow returns, such as a short service, the chops are used against higher-speed attacking shots.

The chop strokes described here are the ones I would use in a range of, say, 6 to 8 feet behind the table, an average depth for defensive play.

THE FOREHAND CHOP

The ready position is shown in *a* of Figure 8. You are standing about 7 feet behind your end of the table. Assume, for the purposes of instruction, that the ball is going to be hit to your forehand side. It will be a medium-speed topspin drive, hit from your opponent's forehand side.

Your first job as the ball approaches is to anticipate, by judging its speed and direction, where its ideal contact point will be. This, of course, is timing, and it is learned through experience and built into a reflex. Your general guide, however, is to remember that on the defensive shots the ideal contact point is lower—farther down on the descending arc —than for the attacking shots. After all, the defender must give the ball time to slow down so that he can handle it more easily. This means retreating from the table and letting the ball fall. The surest choppers try to intercept the ball about thigh high. This entails some fancy footwork on occasion. If his footwork fails and he cannot reach a particular drive so that it falls into its proper place, then the chopper has to improvise, perhaps making contact at his shoestrings or around his shoulders.

But you should be learning with a helper, not an opponent. Continue with the forehand chop shown in Figure 8 and presume the ball will fall where you want it to fall.

57

The Backswing

Position *b* shows the start of the backswing. The wrist begins to draw the top edge of the bat into a cocked position. The bat is not snapped into this position but drawn back gradually and very smoothly throughout the swing. As well as being partially cocked back, the racket is also opened, with its face (on the forehand side) tilted upward.

Positions *b* through *d* show the completion of the backswing. You can see how the face of the racket gets opened during the backswing if you compare *b*, in which only the backhand face of the racket is visible, with *c* and *d*, in which you see only the forehand face of the bat.

Two other points about the backswing:

(1) Throughout the stroke, backswing and forward swing, the elbow is the hinge on which the forearm is swung. The chopping motion is similar to that of scaling a flat stone across a pond. Therefore, the elbow must be held high—and *well out in front* of the hip.

(2) Since the chop is a defensive stroke made as the ball decelerates, the footwork involves a rhythmical retreat from the approaching ball. Figure 8 illustrates the chop made in answer to a medium-speed attack; against harder shots, the retreat of the right foot is more pronounced. As the ball approaches and you make the backswing, your right foot (for the forehand) moves slightly backward and a bit to the right. Your right foot should be planted on a spot that makes further foot adjustments during the forward swing unnecessary. If your right foot has been planted correctly, the ball will fall into a "pocket," from which you can comfortably stroke it out. Anticipation and fluid timing are the keys here; experience is the teacher.

The Forward Swing

Position *e* shows the initiation of the forward swing. Note that the racket is still cocked back and that the elbow is still

58

Figure 8. The Forehand Chop.

d   e   f

j   k   l

bent into a V. Actually, the only indication that the forward swing has begun is the fact that the right shoulder has begun to turn into the ball. There has been an "unpivoting." This also brings the chest squarer to the table. The reason for keeping the forearm and wrist more or less in their original positions is that, by delaying their entry into the stroke until just before impact, the acceleration they will have as they "catch up" during the stroke is increased.

Just before the ball and racket make contact, the wrist and forearm are accelerated. In *i*, the position that was reached just after impact, you can see that the racket head was moved firmly into the bottom surface of the ball. This is the critical moment in the swing, of course. It is the downward blow of the racket head that imparts the spin. Hitting the ball too fully—that is, with too thick a slice— will carry it beyond the table at your opponent's end. Too thin a slice will give you lots of spin, but the ball may not reach the net. You may even fan the ball completely.

The ball should be intercepted above the left foot, not behind the body. Try not to let the ball get behind you. You should be far enough behind *it* to cut it off.

Positions *j* through *l* show the follow-through. The arm is beginning to straighten out; in *l* it is completely straight. Note, too—and this is particularly important—that the head of the racket has gone through the ball. It should not be held back. The bat handle, the forearm and the upper arm are all in a straight line. Players learning the game often compensate for inaccurate timing of the chop by holding back the head of the racket on the forward swing. True, this gives them greater control for that particular return, but the long-range effect can be very damaging. Holding back the wrist can become a bad habit. The wrist and forearm should go through the ball completely. The follow-through is completed with a stop that is almost abrupt. There is still plenty of tension remaining in the hand and forearm. It is as though the forward edge of the bat had been wedged into a sturdy tree.

62

At position *l* the ball should be just about reaching the net. This means that the racket has moved through the ball faster than the ball has carried toward the table. It is similar to taking a golf ball out of a trap with a sand wedge.

THE BACKHAND CHOP

Although the principles of the backhand and the forehand chops are the same, there are differences, which will be discussed later. But first, referring to Figure 9, take a look at the similarities.

Positions *a*, *b* and *c* show the backswing, which consists of two main movements: (1) the turn, or pivot and (2) the arm movement.

The pivot is a smooth turning of the hips and shoulders toward the left. This circular movement revolves around the fixed point, the head. At the completion of the backswing, *c*, the chin is tucked into the right shoulder and the player is drawing a right-eyed bead on the approaching ball.

Linked up with the pivot is the retreating step, this time made with the left foot. Again, the harder the attack, the more pronounced is the retreat of the left foot. From an even weight distribution in the ready position, the weight during the pivot and step moves somewhat to the left side. Not all the weight gets transferred; some weight remains on the right side, supported by the right foot. Note in *d* that the right toe is supporting some weight. What the pivot and partial weight transfer accomplish is to prepare the body for the semicircular uncoiling on the forward swing.

The critical checkpoints on the backswing are these:

(1) The elbow is the hinge, just as it was on the forehand swing. However, on the backhand side it is held much higher. When I make my backhand chop, my elbow is usually pointed toward the target, my opponent's side of the table. In *c* and *d* you can see how far out my elbow is extended and how high I hold it.

63

(2) The purpose of extending the elbow is to gain leverage for the inward swing of the forearm. This leverage is increased by the cocking of the wrist, which takes place smoothly, throughout the entire backswing. In c, my wrist is cocked so that the head of the bat is pointed toward, and almost touching, my collarbone.

Positions d through g illustrate the forward swing. To maintain the tension during this phase, the wrist in d is in a V position relative to the forearm.

If you have pivoted correctly and your timing is good, the forward swing will be merely a reverse of the backswing. At the moment of impact, move your racket (activated by the forearm and wrist, which are uncoiling) down toward the bottom surface of the ball.

Do not make a short, jabbing motion at impact. The contact should be an accident that takes place along the perfectly grooved path of the forward swing, and it should be made around the area of the right hip—in other words, out in front of you.

Note the position of forearm and wrist for the follow-through in g. They have been completely extended. Once again, you must take care not to compensate for poor timing by holding your wrist back, because, while poor timing corrects itself with play, holding the wrist back can develop into a bad habit.

General Notes on Defensive Play

Once you have learned the basic push strokes described in Chapter 4, you are on the way toward developing your defense, for the chops are really extensions of the push. But you must attain ball control with the push shots before you try the longer-range chops. When practicing, make sure that your buddy feeds you serves at one tempo until you have mastered that particular pace. Then go to a faster pace —but remember to check your stroke often to see that backswing and forward swing are correct.

64

Figure 9. The Backhand Chop.

a   b   c   d

e   f   g

Don't try to get too much spin at the beginning. You will probably find, as most starting players do, that when you try to chop, the ball leaves your racket headed for the ceiling. This is not necessarily because the face of your racket is too open, or because you are getting too far under the ball or because you are stroking into the ball at too flat an angle. Adjusting any one of those factors will send the ball back lower, but the best way to adjust the height of the ball is to develop a fine touch so that you can just graze the ball as you stroke through it.

The usual path that the racket takes on the chops is a 45-degree angle; it starts around shoulder height and finishes around hip height. However, this angle changes constantly depending on how far away from the table the ball is taken. For very hard drives that take you way back, you should take the ball lower on its arc with a flatter forward swing. Sometimes I stroke the ball with a perfectly horizontal blade; the face is parallel to the ceiling and the stroke is horizontal, too.

You should have the feeling on these shots that your racket is moving in a fixed path. That path is decided by the backswing. Thus, your bat should take the same angle on the forward swing as on the backswing. The plane of the racket remains the same throughout the stroke.

The stroke is only one aspect of a good defense. Footwork is equally important. You must get to the ball so that you can make the grooved stroke. Think of your stroke as merely a mechanical device that puts the ball on the table automatically when the lever (the racket head) strokes it, remembering that the lever must be in a precise position.

7
The Service

THE SERVICE STROKES are unique, and I have deliberately delayed discussing them because I felt the technique involved would conflict with those for the more important strokes covered in the previous chapters.

In table tennis the serve is nowhere near as important as it is in lawn tennis; the rules simply preclude that. First of all, the ball must bounce on the server's side of the table before it crosses the net; also, the server must hold the ball in the palm of his hand, a flat palm, and throw the ball into the air. He cannot hit the ball off his palm. There is no minimum distance that he must toss the ball, but he must hit the ball *as it descends* from the toss.

These limitations make the serve relatively weak. But not unimportant. Of course, where two players are exactly equal in all other facets of play, the player with the more effective serve will be the winner. For example, if he scores 2 points outright with his serve in every game, this often gives him a winning margin.

But as a general rule, players don't win because of their serves. On the rare occasion that they do, it is at the very highest levels of play only. A few years back, the Chinese and Japanese began using very effective spin serves, which they spent a lot of time practicing. But eventually players gave the service return some attention too, and to a large extent this nullified the effectiveness of these serves.

Beginning and intermediate players should spend very little time trying to cultivate fancy serves. My recommendation is not to spend more than 5 percent of your practice time on serves.

The most important serves are the forehand topspin and the forehand chop.

THE TOPSPIN SERVE

The topspin serve shown in Figure 10 is the serve you make when your intention is to attack on your opponent's return. However, this presumes that a fast serve will force your opponent to make a chop return. In practice, fast topspin serves can usually be returned with a countertopspin (the sponge bat makes this easy), and so frequently the best attacking serve is a short serve close to the net carrying underspin rather than topspin.

In any case, you do need a topspin serve. Position *a* shows that the preparation is similar to that for the forehand drive, but the stroke itself is far different. In this stance, the body is three quarters sideways to the table. The left foot is toward the net, and the knees are slightly bent. The right elbow is close to the hip. At the start of the serve the ball rests on the palm of the left hand. Bat and ball are about 10 inches apart. (See the rules on service, p. 86.)

The toss, made with as smooth a motion as possible, should take the ball about 6 inches into the air from the point it leaves the palm. Too low a toss will force you to

70

Figure 10. The Topspin Serve.

a

b

c

d   e   f

hurry the swing; too high a toss will increase the speed of the falling ball and make it harder to time.

Viewed as a whole, Figure 10 shows that the main difference between the forehand drive and the forehand serve is in the wrist action. In the drive, the head of the bat must be pointed downward prior to contact; on the forehand topspin serve, the wrist moves the racket head parallel to the table surface. The difference is that the drive is essentially an underhand swing, while the serve is a sidearm swing.

On the serve the topspin is applied by rolling the top edge of the bat completely over the top of the ball, and at contact there should be a distinct feeling of wrist tap. This is as close to a slap as you will find in table tennis.

In the follow-through, position *f*, the bat has been taken well across the body, from right to left, whereas in the forehand drive the body pivots with the shot and the racket does not finish across the body.

You can place this serve anywhere on the table, though at the beginning the easiest target is your opponent's forehand—in other words, a cross-court serve from right to left. Also, you can hit it as fast as you want, provided you don't serve off the end of the table. Your speed will develop with your control. Just remember that it is unlikely you will win a point outright with your serve, no matter where you put it or how fast you deliver it. What you can get on the ball is just too limited. Therefore, the serve must be absolutely safe. You should *never* hit it off the table or into the net. Tournament players rarely serve a fault during a season.

THE CHOP SERVE

As I said before, the sponge bat makes it relatively easy to counter a topspin serve with a topspin drive. To avoid this boomerang, many attacking players prefer to use a chop serve, since the slicing, downward blow of the chop restricts

Figure 11. The Chop Serve.

a   b

c   d   e

the forward motion of the ball. The topspin serve, in which the racket meets the ball almost squarely, gives that serve great length.

The ready position is the same as for the topspin serve except that the racket blade is angled backward (in preparation for the downward slice) and the hands are a bit closer together because the swing will be shorter.

Once again, the toss can be about 6 inches, as shown in *b* of Figure 11. The right forearm is brought back to form a tight V with the upper arm. The upper arm, from shoulder to elbow, hangs without tension. Whatever tension there is in this shot—and there is relatively little—is felt in the hand and wrist. Altogether, there is much more wrist action in this shot than on the defensive chops—perhaps because the ball is in a perfect position and control is much less of a problem. This allows you to try for maximum spin.

Therefore, in *c*, the position just before impact, the wrist is cocked and the racket face is open and tilted up. But in *d*, the racket has been released so that the head of the racket is pointed toward the opponent rather than up. In other words, the wrist has *snapped* into the ball.

The follow-through should bring the bottom edge of your racket down until it almost touches the table edge. The path that the racket has taken has been a 45-degree angle.

THE BACKHAND SERVES

Though I have chosen to illustrate the topspin and chop serves on the forehand side, they can be made on the backhand side as well, using the backhand chop and drive as points of departure.

There is no real way of determining on which side a player should develop his serves. There are players whose forehands are all-around stronger than their backhands and yet who choose to serve backhand; the reverse is also true. The decision comes through trial and error.

78

Summary

I HAVE TRIED in the preceding pages to impart a basic understanding of championship technique. The particular emphasis has been on the physical mechanics of the various strokes.

Not all the strokes have been covered, but the ones I have omitted, in order to keep within the scope and prescribed length of this book, are either those that require a highly advanced technique and could not in any case be learned through a text—the loop drive, for example—or those that are comparatively minor and will be developed naturally by the player himself as his level rises—the drop shot, for instance.

Another area that I did not treat is tactics and strategy during match play—in other words, how to play against various styles. This is an important area of knowledge, but it would be more useful to the tournament player than to the average player.

In other words, I have limited this book to basics. Too

often coaching today dwells on unimportant things, such as fancy serves. And then, of course, there is the extravagant preoccupation with sponge switching, the frantic search for the magic rubber that will instantaneously turn the player into a world champion.

Undeniably, physical conditioning, keen tactics and good equipment are important, but you must also maintain a proper perspective. If not, you tend to overlook the fundamentals. Traveling to tournaments around the United States, as I do each season, I am always dismayed to see how few of our juniors, hardworking though they are, have any chance at all of reaching a top world ranking. They have the talent, but most of the time some basic violation of theory became incorporated into their games when they began. Worse, they are unaware of it. Worse still, in their passionate optimism that very soon they will break through, they would probably scoff at a coach who said, "Look here, your grip is wrong by a whole quarter of an inch. You'll never be able to hit a solid forehand drive holding the bat that way."

Therefore, fellow addict, beginner, intermediate or near-ranking player, pay attention to fundamentals. Playing the game with style, with good form, is plainly and simply more enjoyable. And in the long run you will win more matches too.

International Laws of Table Tennis

1. The Table

The table shall be in surface rectangular, 9 ft. in length, 5 ft. in width; it shall be supported in such a way that its upper surface shall be 2 ft. 6 in. above the floor, and shall lie in a horizontal plane.

It shall be made of any material and shall yield a uniform bounce of not less than 8¾ in. and not more than 9¾ in. when a standard ball, preferably of medium bounce, is dropped from a height of 12 in. above its surface.

The upper surface of the table shall be termed the "playing surface"; it shall be matt, colour very dark, preferably dark green, with a white line ¾ in. broad along each edge.

The lines at the edges or ends of the playing surface shall be termed "end lines." The lines at the edges or sides of the playing surface shall be termed "side lines."

2. The Net and Its Supports

The playing surface shall be divided into two courts of equal size by a net running parallel to the end lines and 4 ft. 6 in. from each. The net, with its suspension, shall be 6 ft. in length; its upper part along its whole length shall be 6 in. above the playing surface; its lower part along the whole length shall be close to the playing surface. The net shall be suspended by a cord attached at each end to an upright post 6 in. high; the outside limits of each post shall be 6 in. outside the side line.

3. The Ball

The ball shall be spherical. It shall be made of celluloid or a similar plastic, white or yellow and matt; it shall not be less than 1.46 in. nor more than 1.50 in. in diameter; it shall not be less than 2.40 gr. nor more than 2.53 gr. in weight.

4. The Racket

The racket may be of any size, shape, or weight. Its surface shall be dark coloured and matt. The blade shall be continuous, of even thickness, flat and rigid. If the blade is covered on either side, this covering may be either—
of plain, ordinary pimpled rubber, with pimples outward, of a total thickness of not more than 2 mm.; or—
of "sandwich," consisting of a layer of cellular rubber surfaced by plain ordinary pimpled rubber—turned outwards or inwards—in which case the total thickness of covering of either side shall not be more than 4 mm.

When rubber is used on both sides of a racket, the colour need not be similar: when wood is used for either side, or for both sides, it should be dark, either naturally, or by being stained (not painted) in such a way as not to change the friction-character of its surface.

Note: The part of the blade nearest the handle and gripped by the fingers may be covered with cork or other materials for convenience of grip; it is to be regarded as part of the handle.

Note: If the reverse side of the racket is never used for striking the ball, it may all be of cork or any other material convenient for gripping. The limitation of racket cover materials refers only to the striking surface. A stroke with a side covered with cork or any other gripping surface would, however, be illegal and result in a lost point.

Note: Each side of the blade, whether used for striking the ball or not, must be of a uniform dark colour.

5. The Order of Play: Definitions

The player who first strikes the ball during a rally shall be termed the server.

The player who next strikes the ball during a rally shall be termed the receiver.

The server shall first make a good service, the receiver shall then make a good return, and thereafter server and receiver shall each alternately make a good return.

The period during which the ball is in play shall be termed a rally.

A rally the result of which is not scored shall be termed a let.

A rally the result of which is scored shall be termed a point.

6. A Good Service

The ball shall be placed on the palm of the free hand, which must be stationary, open and flat, and above the level of the playing surface. Service shall commence by the server projecting the ball by hand only, without imparting spin, near vertically upwards (see diagram), so that the ball is visible at all times to the umpire, and so that it visibly leaves the palm. As the ball is then descending from the height of its trajectory, it shall be struck so that it touch first the server's court and then, passing directly over or around the net, touch the receiver's court.

The New Service Rule Adopted for Use as from July 1, 1967

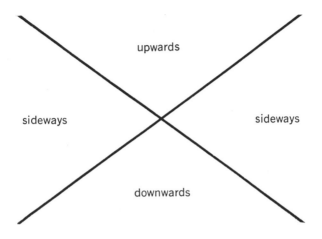

upwards

sideways   sideways

downwards

Note: Missed Service: Note that, if a player, in attempting to serve, miss the ball altogether, it is a lost point because the ball was in play from the moment it left his hand and a good service has not been made of the ball already in play.

Definitions for above:

"Struck": "Struck" means "hit with the racket or with the racket hand" which, for this purpose, shall be understood as included in the racket. The racket hand is the hand carrying the racket; the free open hand is the hand not carrying the racket. Therefore, a return effected with the hand alone, after dropping the racket, is "not good" for it is no longer the "racket hand"; a return effected by the racket alone, after it has slipped or been thrown from the hand, is likewise "not good," for the ball is not "struck."

The phrase Table Surface (comprising the courts) is to be interpreted as including the top edges of the table-top, and a ball in play which strikes these latter is therefore good and still in play; though if it strikes the side of the table-top below the edge, it becomes dead and counts against the last striker.

The direction in which the ball is travelling since it was last struck, its spin, and the direction in which it rebounds from the edge can all help to distinguish between a "good" ball that has touched the edge and a "bad" ball that has made contact below the edge. If the point of contact of the ball has occurred at the end or side of the table away from the striker it must nearly always have been a "good" touch; only exceptionally heavy spin could have brought about a contact completely below the edge. If the contact has occurred on the same side of the table as that from which the ball was struck, it may, however, have occurred below the edge and if the rebound in this case is directly downward this is a sign that the contact must have been "bad," i.e. against the side, below the edge.

If the ball, in passing over the net, or around the net, touch it or its supports it shall, nevertheless, be considered to have passed directly. "Around the net" shall be considered as being under or around the projection of the net and supports outside the side line. The net end should be close enough to the post to prevent the ball from passing between net and post and to pass so would not constitute "around the net."

The free hand, while in contact with the ball in service, shall be open, with the fingers together, thumb free and the ball resting on the palm without being cupped or pinched in any way by the fingers.

7. A Good Return

A ball having been served or returned in play shall be struck so that it pass directly over or around the net and touch directly the opponent's court, provided that, if the ball, having been served or returned in play, return with its own impetus over or around the net, it may be struck, while still in play, so that it touch directly the opponent's court.

8. In Play

The ball is in play from the moment at which it is projected from the hand in service until:—

It has touched one court twice consecutively.

It has, except in service, touched each court alternately without having been struck by the racket intermediately.

It has been struck by either player more than once consecutively.

It has touched either player or anything that he wears or carries, except his racket or his racket hand below the wrist.

On the volley it come in contact with the racket or the racket hand below the wrist.

It has touched any object other than the net, supports, or those referred to above.

It has, under the Expedite System, been returned by thirteen successive good returns of the receiving player or pair.

9. A Let

The rally is a let:—

If the ball served in passing over the net touch it or its supports, provided the service either be otherwise good or be volleyed by the receiver.

Definition: The Volley: If the ball in play come into contact with the racket or racket hand, not yet having touched the playing surface on one side of the net since last being struck on the other side, it shall be said to have been volleyed.

If a service be delivered when the receiver is not ready, provided always that he may not be deemed to be unready if he attempt to strike at the ball.

If either player be prevented by an accident, not under his control, from serving a good service or making a good return.

If either player lose the point owing to an accident not within his control.

If it be interrupted for correction of a mistake in playing order or ends.

If it be interrupted for application of the Expedite System.

If it be interrupted by the intrusion of another ball in the playing area.

Ball Fractured in Play

If the ball split or become otherwise fractured in play, affecting a player's return, the rally is a let. It is the umpire's duty to stop play, recording a let, when he has reason to believe that the ball in play is fractured or imperfect; and to decide those cases in which the faulty ball is clearly fractured in actually going out of play, and in no way handicaps the player's return, when the point should be scored. In all cases of doubt, however, he should declare a let.

10. A Point

Either player shall lose a point:—

If he fail to make a good service.

If a good service or a good return having been made by his opponent, he fail to make a good return.

If he, or his racket, or anything that he wears or carries touch the net or its supports while the ball is in play.

If he, or his racket, or anything that he wears or carries, move the playing surface while the ball is in play.

If his free hand touch the playing surface while the ball is in play.

If, before the ball in play shall have passed over the end lines or side lines not yet having touched the playing surface on his side of the table since being struck by his opponent, it come in contact with him or with anything that he wears or carries.

If at any time he volley the ball.

Expedite System

If a game be unfinished fifteen minutes after it has begun, the rest of that game and the remaining games of the match shall proceed under the Expedite System. Thereafter, each player shall serve one service in turn and, if the service and twelve following strokes of the server are returned by good returns of the receiver, the server shall lose the point.

If time was called during a rally, the player who served that rally shall serve first. If time was called between rallies, the receiver of the last rally shall serve next.

11. A Game

A game shall be won by the player who first wins 21 points, unless both players shall have scored 20 points, when the winner of the game shall be he who first wins two points more than his opponent.

12. A Match

A match shall consist of one game or the best of three or best of five games.

Play shall be continuous throughout, except that either opposing player is entitled to claim a repose period of not more than five minutes' duration between the third and fourth games of a five-game match, and of one minute between any other successive games.

Note: This rule defines a contest between two players or pairs. A contest consisting of a group of individual matches between two sides is usually distinguished as a "team match."

13. The Choice of Ends and Service

The choice of ends and the right to be server or receiver in every match shall be decided by toss, provided that, if the winner of the toss choose the right to be server or receiver, the other player shall have the choice of ends, and vice-versa, and provided that the winner of the toss may, if he prefer it, require the other player to make the first choice.

14. The Change of Ends and Service

Ends

The player who started at one end in a game shall start at the other in the immediately subsequent game, and so on, until the end of the match. In the last possible game of the match the players shall change ends when first either player reaches the score 10.

Service

After five points the receiver shall become the server, and the server the receiver, and so on after each five points until the end of the game or the score 20-all, or if the game be interrupted under the Expedite System. From the score 20-all, or if the game be interrupted under the Expedite System, the service shall change after each point until the end of the game. The player who served first in a game shall be receiver first in the immediately subsequent game, and so on until the end of a match.

15. Out of Order of Ends or Service

Ends

If the players have not changed ends when ends should have been changed, the players shall change ends as soon as the mistake is discovered, unless a game has been completed since the error, when the error shall be ignored. In any circumstances, all points scored before the discovery shall be reckoned.

Service

If a player serve out of his turn, play shall be interrupted as soon as the mistake is discovered and shall continue with that player serving who, according to the sequence established at the beginning of the match, should be the server at the score that has been reached. In any circumstances, all points scored before the discovery shall be reckoned.

DOUBLES

16. The above Laws shall apply in the Doubles Game except as below.

17. The Table

The surface of the table shall be divided into two parts by a white line ⅛ in. broad, running parallel with the side lines and distant equally from each of them. This line shall be termed the centre line.

Note: The doubles centre line may be permanently marked in full length on the table. This is a convenience and in no way invalidates the table for singles play.

The part of the table surface on the nearer side of the net and the right of the centre line in respect to the server shall be called the server's right half-court, that on the left in respect to him the server's left half-court. The part of the table surface on the farther side of the net and the left of the centre line in respect to the server shall be called the receiver's right half-court, that on the right in respect to the server the receiver's left half-court.

18. A Good Service

The service shall be delivered as otherwise provided, and so that it touch first the server's right half-court or the centre line on his side of the net, and then passing directly over or around the net, touch the receiver's right half-court or the centre line on his side of the net.

19. The Order of Play

The server shall first make a good service, the receiver shall then make a good return, the partner of the server shall then make a good return, the partner of the receiver shall then make a good return, the server shall then make a good return and thereafter each player alternately in that sequence shall make a good return.

20. The Choice of the Order of Play

The pair who have the right to serve the first five services in any game shall decide which partner shall do so. In the first game of a match the opposing pair shall then decide similarly which shall be the first receiver. In subsequent games the serving pair shall choose their first server and the first receiver will then be established automatically to correspond with the first server as provided below.

21. The Order of Service

Throughout each game, except as provided in the second paragraph, the first five services shall be delivered by the selected partner of the pair who have the right to do so and shall be received by the appropriate partner of the opposing pair. The second five services shall be delivered by the receiver of the first five services and received by the partner of the server of the first five services. The third five services shall be delivered by the partner of the server of the first five services and received by the partner of the receiver of the first five services. The fourth five services shall be delivered by the partner of the receiver of the first five services and received by the server of the first five services. The fifth five services shall be delivered as the first five services. And so on, in sequence, until the end of the game or the score 20-all or the introduction of the Expedite System, when the sequence of serving and receiving shall be uninterrupted, but each player shall serve only one service in turn until the end of the game.

In the last possible game of a match when first either player reaches the score 10 the receiving pair must alter its order of serving.

In each game of a match the initial order of receiving shall be opposite to that in the preceding game.

22. Out of Order of Receiving

If a player act as receiver out of his turn play shall be interrupted as soon as the mistake is discovered and shall continue with that player receiving who, according to the sequence established at the beginning of the game or at the score 10 if that sequence has been changed, should be receiver at the score which has been reached. In any circumstances all points scored before the discovery shall be reckoned.